ENGLAND

 **Marshall Cavendish**
Benchmark

New York

This edition first published in 2011 in
the United States of America by
Marshall Cavendish Benchmark.

Marshall Cavendish Benchmark
99 White Plains Road
Tarrytown, NY 10591
Website: www.marshallcavendish.us

© Marshall Cavendish International (Asia)
Pte Ltd 2011
Originated and designed by Marshall Cavendish
International (Asia) Pte Ltd
A member of Times Publishing Limited
Times Centre, 1 New Industrial Road
Singapore 536196

Written by: Harlinah Whyte
Edited by: Crystal Chan
Designed by: Lock Hong Liang
Picture research: Thomas Khoo

Library of Congress Cataloging-in-Publication Data
Whyte, Harlinah.
England / by Harlinah Whyte.
p. cm. -- (Festivals of the world)
Includes bibliographical references and index.
Summary: "This book explores the exciting culture
and many festivals that are celebrated in England"--
Provided by publisher.
ISBN 978-1-60870-098-1
1. Festivals--England--Juvenile literature.
2. England--Social life and customs--
Juvenile literature. I. Title.
GT4843.W49 2011
394.26942--dc22
2010000310
ISBN 978-1-60870-098-1

Printed in Malaysia

1 3 6 5 4 2

Contents

It's Festival Time . . .

From the colorful costumes of the Notting Hill Carnival to the burning of the dummy on Guy Fawkes Day, England has many fascinating celebrations. Some of England's festivals go back thousands of years, and others were brought to the country more recently from around the world. Come and dance around the Maypole, put on a carnival mask, and meet the queen. It's festival time in England!

Where's England?

Located in western Europe, England is part of the island of Great Britain in the United Kingdom. The country is famous for its green countryside, but most English people live in big cities. The capital of the United Kingdom is London.

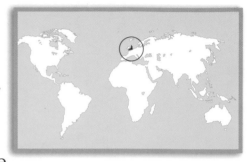

England was once the center of the British Empire, which included large areas of North America, Africa, Asia, and Australia. Most of these areas are now made up of independent nations.

Who Are the English?

Some of the original inhabitants of the island were the **Celts** [kelts]. More than two thousand years ago, many Celts were driven out of England by Roman invaders. Over the centuries, the few Celts who remained mixed with the invaders to form the modern English people. In more recent years, people have come to England from former British colonies, such as India, Pakistan, and parts of the Caribbean.

✳ These schoolgirls are examples of the people who live in England.

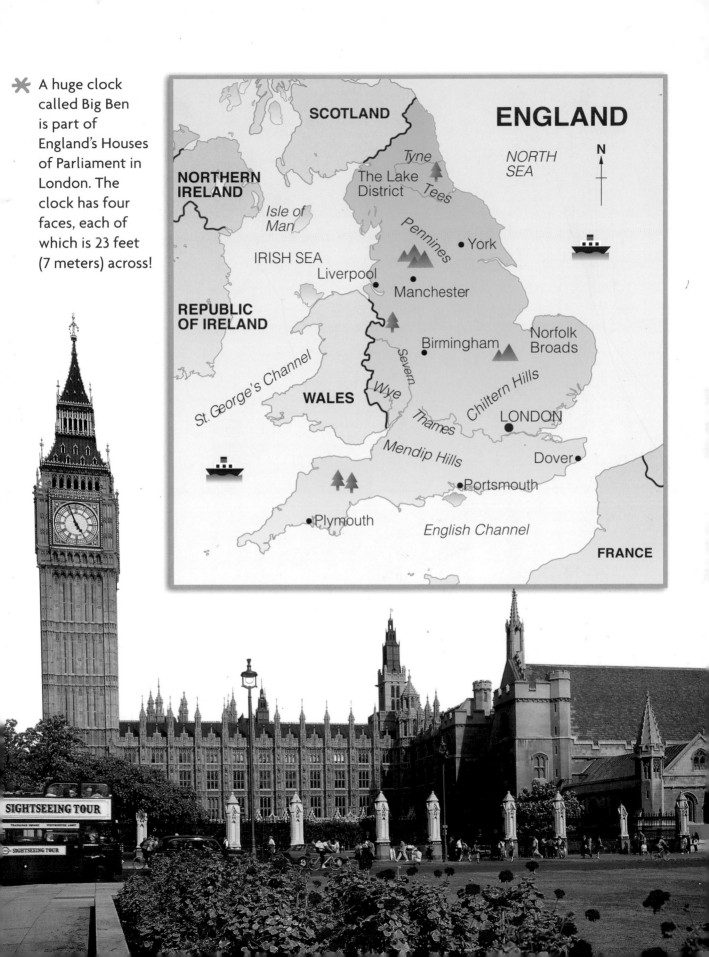

A huge clock called Big Ben is part of England's Houses of Parliament in London. The clock has four faces, each of which is 23 feet (7 meters) across!

SCOTLAND

ENGLAND

NORTHERN IRELAND

NORTH SEA

Tyne

The Lake District

Tees

Isle of Man

Pennines

York

IRISH SEA

Liverpool

Manchester

REPUBLIC OF IRELAND

St. George's Channel

Severn

Birmingham

Norfolk Broads

WALES

Wye

Thames

Chiltern Hills

LONDON

Mendip Hills

Dover

Portsmouth

Plymouth

English Channel

FRANCE

SIGHTSEEING TOUR
SIGHTSEEING TOUR

What Are the Festivals?

SPRING

✳ **Pancake Day**—The Tuesday before Lent when people traditionally eat pancakes and take part in pancake races.

✳ **Easter**—Celebrates Jesus Christ's return to life and springtime.

✳ **May Day**—A springtime festival in which people dance around a tall pole.

✳ **Beltane**—A period of festivities that marks the beginning of summer.

Looking for some pomp and ceremony? Come celebrate the Queen's birthday!

SUMMER

✳ **Notting Hill Carnival**—A colorful summer fiesta that has its roots in the Caribbean islands.

✳ **Village Fairs**—Village gatherings that include agricultural shows and contests for charity.

✳ **Harvest Festivals**—Churches are decorated with crops to give thanks for the summer harvest.

✳ **Queen's Official Birthday**—Queen Elizabeth II's day of birth, which is recognized as a public holiday.

✳ **Dressing the Wells**—Flowers are placed next to wells to give thanks for the water supply.

Put on your costume and dancing shoes for the Notting Hill Carnival!

I'm Friar Tuck! Come meet me and my friend Robin Hood at the May Day games.

AUTUMN

✳ **Guy Fawkes Day**—A day to remember the failed attempt of Guy Fawkes to blow up the Houses of Parliament.

✳ **London to Brighton Vintage Car Rally**—A car race for cars built before 1905.

✳ **Lord Mayor's Day**—The new Lord Mayor of London takes office after a grand city parade.

✳ **Halloween**—The evening of October 31 when children dress in costumes.

✳ **Armistice Day**—People wear red poppies and observe two minutes of silence to remember the soldiers who died in World War I and World War II.

✳ **Pearly Kings and Queens**—Londoners dress in black clothing covered with pearly white buttons.

WINTER

✳ **Hanukkah**—This holiday is observed by the Jewish community in England, who celebrate their faith by lighting special candles for eight nights in a row.

✳ **Christmas**—People celebrate the birth of Jesus by exchanging gifts and decorating a tree.

✳ **New Year's Day**—The first day of the calendar year.

✳ **Chelsea Pensioners' Parade**—Veterans from the Royal Hospital Chelsea take part in a grand parade held in their honor.

✳ **Chinese New Year**—People gather in the streets to watch lion and dragon dances and to set off fireworks.

Easter

Easter is one of the most important festivals in the Christian calendar. It is the day when Christians celebrate Jesus Christ, the religion's founder, and his resurrection, or return to life. However, Easter began as an ancient festival of spring.

From Eostre to Easter

One of the groups of invaders that came to England hundreds of years ago were the **Anglo-Saxons.** They brought many of their customs with them. One of their customs was to celebrate the coming of spring at the end of the long, cold winter. Their goddess of spring was called **Eostre** [EAST-er]. Over time, the Anglo-Saxons became Christians. They worshiped Jesus Christ, but they never stopped practicing their old traditions. Many of the Easter traditions celebrated in England today, such as giving eggs and Easter bunnies, come from the Anglo-Saxon festival. In fact, even the name of the holiday was handed down by the Anglo-Saxons.

Eggs and Rabbits

Why are eggs eaten at Easter, and where did the Easter bunny come from? In the Anglo-Saxon tradition, the coming of spring was a time to celebrate new life. Eggs and rabbits are Anglo-Saxon symbols of life and birth. Even though most people no longer know the meaning behind these symbols, they still enjoy eating chocolate eggs and bunnies at Easter time!

Hot Cross Buns

Hot cross buns were also introduced by the Anglo-Saxons. During the spring festival, an ox was sacrificed to the gods for a good harvest. Afterward, people celebrated by eating cakes with the mark of ox horns on top. The English word *bun* comes from the Anglo-Saxon word for ox. Later, the mark of the ox horns was thought to represent the sign of the cross, an important Christian symbol.

✱ The first one to roll an Easter egg to the end of the path will win this egg-rolling race!

Celebrating Easter

*Searching for hidden eggs in the garden is one of the most exciting parts of Easter.

The Friday before Easter Sunday is called Good Friday. The day before Good Friday, the Queen of England hands out special coins to the poor. Each year she hands out an extra coin because the number of coins is based on her age.

Good Friday is the day for feasting on delicious hot cross buns. Most Christians go to church on Good Friday, and some pray for as long as three hours. Easter Sunday, however, is a day for fun. There are Easter egg hunts, egg-rolling contests, and lots of chocolate. Many people also perform plays that tell the story of Easter.

*Queen Elizabeth II has been the Queen of England since 1952. In this picture, she is shown attending a special Easter church service.

Pancake Day

In the past, Christians fasted for the forty days leading up to Easter. This period is called Lent. Some people still try to avoid eating rich foods, such as butter and eggs, during Lent. So, on Shrove Tuesday, the day before Lent begins, they use up all of their eggs and butter making pancakes! This is a popular celebration called Pancake Day. On this day, families get together to eat pancakes. English people like to eat pancakes drizzled with lemon juice and sugar instead of syrup. In English villages, people compete in pancake races. They run while tossing a pancake in a frying pan. Although it is a long time before Easter, many people in England think of Pancake Day as the beginning of the Easter celebration.

✳ These women are taking part in a pancake race. The competitors must be careful not to drop the pancakes as they run.

THINK ABOUT THIS

According to an English legend, the pancake race was started more than five hundred years ago by a woman making pancakes. When she heard the church bells ringing and discovered she was late for church, she dashed out of the house with her frying pan and ran all the way to the church.

May Day

May 1 is a public holiday in many countries. In some countries, it is known as Labor Day, a workers' holiday. In England, May 1 is called May Day, and it is a time to celebrate the beginning of summer.

Reviving the Past

The Celtic people of ancient England split the year into two seasons— winter and summer. The first day of May marked the start of summer. On this day, a great festival was held to honor the Sun. This festival was called *Beltane*, meaning fire of God.

As Christianity spread across Europe, the May festival became a time for farmers to celebrate the start of the growing season. Summer was the time when crops thrived and animals had plenty to eat. Today people in England celebrate May Day with many of the traditional dances and ceremonies of Beltane.

✳ These girls are dressed up for the May Day celebration.

* Morris dancing always attracts a crowd of curious onlookers.

Let's Dance!

Everyone knows it's May Day when they see **Morris dancers**! You can tell who they are by their bright clothing, the flowers on their hats, and the bells on their legs. They wave ribbons, colored sticks, and bright scarves. The dances were traditionally performed by men to frighten away bad spirits. Today women also join in the fun of the Morris dance. Sometimes the dancers wear animal masks, and there is often a person dressed as a "hobby horse." A huge crowd gathers around the hobby horse to watch it perform silly tricks. All day long people walk through the streets to watch the dancing and enjoy the party.

Round the Maypole

In villages and towns throughout England, dancing around the Maypole is a favorite part of May Day. The dance is taken directly from Beltane. After cutting down a tree and stripping off the branches, long, brightly colored ribbons are tied to the top of the trunk. Each dancer holds a ribbon and skips around the pole. They move in and out so that the ribbons weave together. Today Maypole dancing is especially popular with children.

* People dance around the Maypole.

* Opposite: Robin Hood is still part of many May Day festivals. People dress as characters from the legend and enjoy playing games, such as shooting arrows.

Robin Hood's Day

The folk hero Robin Hood is extremely popular in England. Hundreds of years ago, his story became part of the May Day celebrations. As the village festival became widespread in English cities, it expanded to include singers, plays, archery competitions, and the choosing of a May King and May Queen. The May King dressed as Robin Hood, and the May Queen dressed as Maid Marian. Other people dressed as Robin Hood's merry men. In some places, May Day is still known as Robin Hood's Day.

THINK ABOUT THIS
Some old Celtic festivals are still celebrated by people in England. These people are called Druids after the ancient Celtic priests and teachers.

Royal Pageantry

One of the special things about England is its royal family. Most English people enjoy the traditions that go with having a king or queen. The royal family's schedule is listed in the newspaper every day, and there are many public occasions when people can see members of the royal family.

There are also events with officials, such as the Lord Mayor of London. Even though Queen Elizabeth II does not have the same power as kings and queens who lived centuries ago, royal **pageantry** has kept its splendor, tradition, and richness.

✱ Even the horses wear rich and gorgeous costumes for royal events.

Trooping the Color

The queen's birthday is in April, but since it falls close to Easter, it is officially celebrated in June. On a Saturday in June, the queen and other members of the royal family ride on horseback or in royal stagecoaches to Horse Guards, an old stone building with a large parade ground. There the queen inspects her personal guard. The display of troops is called Trooping the Color. Each **regiment** carries its own color, or special flag. The beautiful uniforms, soldiers on horseback, and rows of marching troops make this a very grand occasion. Thousands of people gather in the streets to watch the queen's parade go by. There is not enough room for everyone to see the display at Horse Guards, so only a limited number of tickets are given away.

✳ It takes a lot of practice to get all these soldiers to march together.

✳ A Horse Guard on duty.

Lord Mayor's Day

One of the most spectacular ceremonies in all of England is Lord Mayor's Day. Each year, a new Lord Mayor is elected to represent the city of London. In fact, this tradition has been going on for more than nine hundred years. On the second Saturday of November, the Lord Mayor dresses in special clothes and parades through London in a stagecoach. The coach is drawn by six horses. The twelve great city **livery companies** follow the coach in decorated floats.

✳ Queen Elizabeth II with her husband, Prince Philip, Duke of Edinburgh, and the Lord Mayor of London, attend a service at St. Paul's Cathedral in 2002. The service was part of the queen's Golden Jubilee, which celebrated her fifty-year rule as queen of the United Kingdom.

Chelsea Pensioners Parade

Every February 16 there is a parade at the Royal Hospital Chelsea. This is a special hospital that looks after veterans, soldiers who have fought in wars. The hospital was founded by King Charles II and is more than three hundred years old. Many of the veterans, who are known as Chelsea Pensioners, are over eighty years old. On their parade day, they wear red uniforms and all the medals they have won. As a special honor, they are greeted by a member of the royal family.

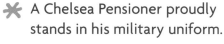

* A Chelsea Pensioner proudly stands in his military uniform.

Notting Hill Carnival

Since the 1950s, people from the Caribbean islands have been coming to live in England. Over the years, the Caribbean people have made very important cultural contributions. One of the most exciting is the Notting Hill Carnival, which takes place in London every year.

Carnival Time!

The tradition of carnival started centuries ago as a huge celebration in January or February. In the Caribbean islands, the weather is warm at this time of year, and the carnival was celebrated outdoors. When immigrants came to England from the Caribbean, they missed their carnival. So in August 1961, the people of Notting Hill in London held the first summer carnival. It was a great success, and the crowds have been flocking to the Notting Hill Carnival ever since.

* Hundreds of people dress in amazing costumes like these at the Notting Hill Carnival.

The Big Party

The Notting Hill Carnival is a wonderful party! Men, women, and children dress up in elaborate costumes that sometimes take weeks to make. They dance through the streets in groups or ride on decorated floats. The groups of costumed dancers are called **mas** [MUSS] **bands**. *Mas* is short for masquerade. People from across England come to watch the mas bands. Sidewalk stalls serve all kinds of Caribbean specialties, such as goat curry.

✳ This musician is beating a steel drum made from an old oil barrel.

THINK ABOUT THIS

Do you like to dress up in fancy costumes and masks? Can you think of any other holidays when people dress up and wear masks?

Steel Bands and Calypso

At carnival time, the streets are filled with the sound of steel drums and **calypso** [ca-LIP-so]. Calypso is a popular type of music from the Caribbean.

The lively calypso melodies are played by steel drum bands. Steel drums were originally made from old oil barrels. A hammer was used to beat the end of the barrel into a curved drum head. Different notes are produced by striking different parts of the drum head. Even today each steel drum is made by hand. Calypso and steel band music are part of the carnival's celebration of Caribbean culture. The drums also produce wonderful music!

✳ Mas bands compete to see who can come up with the most spectacular costumes, the best dance moves, and the most interesting theme.

Guy Fawkes Day

On November 5, the English celebrate a holiday unique to their country. Huge bonfires are built, dummies are burned on the fires, and fireworks are set off all over England.

The Gunpowder Plot

In 1605 a group of Catholics led by Guy Fawkes tried to blow up the Houses of Parliament and kill King James. They were angry at the way the king treated Catholics. They hoped that by killing the king they could take control of the country. Fawkes and his men rolled thirty-six barrels of gunpowder under the Houses of Parliament. At the last moment the king was warned, and Guy Fawkes and his men were captured. Today people remember this day with a rhyme:

Remember, remember, the fifth of November,
Gunpowder, treason, and plot.
We see no reason
Why gunpowder treason
Should ever be forgot!

Burning the Guy

Bonfires have been an important part of English festivals since the time of the Celts. Guy Fawkes Day is sometimes known as Bonfire Night. On Bonfire Night, people from neighborhoods, villages, and towns get together to watch the burning of a representation of Guy Fawkes. The dummy that is burned is made of old clothes stuffed with straw, newspaper, or rags. The dummy is simply called the **guy**.

In the evening, some children walk in the streets carrying the dummy and begging for "a penny for the guy." The children often use the money to buy firecrackers to set off during the night. A huge fireworks display completes the evening.

✳ On Guy Fawkes Day, children have fun waving sparklers.

Things for You to Do

Do you celebrate the end of winter? After months of cold weather, it's good to see flowers, green grass, and blue skies. On May Day, English children like to celebrate with dancing and flowers. Here are some things you can do to make spring special.

Dance Around a Maypole

An English May Day celebration is not complete without a Maypole. Making one is easy. Attach some ribbons to a pole stuck in the ground or to a slender tree. You and your friends can each hold a ribbon and dance around singing:

Now we go round the Maypole high,
Maypole high, Maypole high.
Now we go round the Maypole high,
Let the colored ribbons fly!

Make a May Basket

Spring is the time for flowers. In some parts of England, children secretly deliver flowers to their friends and neighbors on May Day. They leave a small basket of flowers on the doorstep or hang them from the doorknob. You can make your own May basket. Shape a semicircle of paper into a cone, and glue or tape the seam. Punch holes in the sides and tie a piece of ribbon through the holes. Decorate the cone with paint, markers, or colorful pieces of paper. Before putting fresh flowers into the cone, wrap the stems with damp paper towel and enclose the ends of the stems in a small plastic bag. This will keep the flowers fresh and stop the cone from getting wet. Now you can give your May Day flower basket to someone special!

FURTHER INFORMATION

Books: *England A–Z.* Byron Augustin (Children's Press, 2006).
England: The Culture. Erinn Banting and Carolyn Black (Crabtree Publishing, 2004).
English Folktales. Dan Keding and Amy Douglas (Libraries Unlimited, 2005).
The Twelve Days of Christmas. Gennady Spirin (Marshall Cavendish Benchmark, 2009).
Websites: http://projectbritain.com—A vibrant and engaging website that gives the reader useful information about England, Scotland, and Wales.
www.visitbritain.us/about-britain/history-and-culture/—Includes interesting information about England's history, government, religion, and culture.
www.enjoyengland.com/attractions/—A reader-friendly guide that provides information, tips, and advice on the best places to explore in England.

Make a Guy

On Guy Fawkes Day, every bonfire needs a guy. These stuffed figures represent Guy Fawkes, one of the men who tried to blow up the Houses of Parliament. One guy can look very different from another—there is no right way to make one. You can make a guy using old clothes of any kind, and you can give it any face you like.

You will need:

1. A long-sleeved shirt
2. A pair of long pants
3. A pillowcase
4. Newspaper
5. A hat
6. A marker
7. String
8. A stapler

1 Stuff the shirt, pants, and pillowcase with crumpled newspaper. Tie off the pillowcase and the arms and legs with string.

2 Use the marker to draw a face on the pillowcase.

3 To assemble the guy, lay out the head, body, and legs. Tuck the pillowcase into the shirt. Staple the bottom of the pillowcase to the top of the shirt. Then staple the shirt to the pants. Give your guy a hat, and he's ready to go!

Make Scones

English people enjoy scones as an afternoon snack, often with a cup of tea. Scones are delicious with jam and whipped cream, or just plain butter. They're best when they're freshly baked and still warm. This recipe makes about twelve scones.

You will need:

1. 2-1/2 cups (280 g) self-rising flour
2. 1/3 cup (65 g) butter, cut into small pieces
3. 1/3 cup (65 g) sugar
4. 4 tablespoons milk
5. Pinch of salt
6. Extra flour
7. A mixing bowl
8. A sifter
9. A wooden spoon
10. Measuring cups
11. A board
12. A rolling pin
13. A round cutter
14. A baking tray
15. A wire rack
16. Potholders
17. Measuring spoons

1 Wash your hands, and then sift the flour and salt into a mixing bowl to get rid of any lumps. Rub the butter into the flour with your fingertips until the mixture is like bread crumbs.

2 Add the sugar and milk and gently squeeze the mixture into a ball using your fingers.

3 Roll the mixture out onto a floured board until it is about 3/4 inch (2 cm) thick.

4 Cut circles out of the mixture with a round cutter. Put them onto a greased baking tray. With an adult's help, bake your scones at 425°F (220°C) for about 10 minutes, or until brown on top. Leave them to cool on a rack.

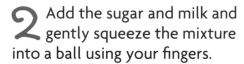

Glossary

Anglo-Saxons	The Angles and Saxons, tribes from Denmark and Germany who settled in England nearly 1,500 years ago.
calypso	A popular Caribbean musical form.
Celts	Early peoples who lived in Great Britain.
Eostre	The Anglo-Saxon goddess of spring.
guy	A dummy made of old clothes that is burned on a bonfire.
livery companies	Traditional trade and craft associations in London.
mas bands	Groups of dancers who parade through the streets during the Notting Hill Carnival.
Morris dancers	Traditional dancers at the May Day celebrations.
pageantry	Grand, formal displays and ceremonies.
regiment	An organized unit of soldiers.

Index